Endorsements

"Nothing can fully describe the pain and the loss suffered by a person who is taking care of a loved one who has succumbed to the awful ravages of Alzheimer's. Yet there is a way to mitigate that pain, through a rich and deep understanding of the disease itself.

"One can acquire such an understanding from clinical reports and academic treaties on the subject--but no one can explain it quite like someone who has lived with the disease and watched it affect a dearly loved other.

"Petra Gerda Paul is such a person--and she found a remarkable way to heal herself from the trauma of taking care of her beloved husband through years of his struggle with this disease.

"Bravely looking at all of her experiences, she has created this account, which may give new understanding--and therefore an easier path--for other Alzheimer's caregivers.

"I am grateful to Petra for her contribution to a field where clarification and more experiential insights are badly needed."

~ Neale Donald Walsch, author of
Conversations with God

"*In* Letters to My Immortal Beloved, *Petra Paul has captured the essence of what it is to be a caregiver for a loved one who has Alzheimer's disease; I know, I went through it with my mother. This book--tiny, but mighty-- is more than a journal, more than a collection of love letters, it is a testament to love, commitment, strength, and faith. I hope everyone dealing with the impact that Alzheimer's has on the lives of everyone involved will have the opportunity to read this, to gather strength and comfort from it, and--most of all--to know that YES, they will come through it to the other side. Thank you, Petra, for this testament to the power of love.*"

~ Rev. Susan Overland, Assistant Minister,
Center for Spiritual Living, San Jose, CA

"*Reading Petra's book shows me that it's never too late to meet your soul mate, and that love gives us the strength to survive even an ordeal like Alzheimer's disease caregiving. Petra's husband was cared for in our Memory Care Community in his final days.*"

Scott Evans, Executive Director
San Carlos Elms

Letters to My Immortal Beloved:

My Journey from Heaven on Earth Through Alzheimer's and Back

Petra Gerda Paul

Letters to My Immortal Beloved:
My Journey from Heaven on Earth
Through Alzheimer's and Back

Copyright @ 2013

Letters to My Immortal Beloved may be purchased through book dealers and online bookstores and at www.SacredLife.com.

ISBN: 978-09896593-0-7
ISBN: 0989659305
Library of Congress Control Number: 2013944646

The information, ideas, and suggestions in this book are not intended as a substitute for professional advice. Before following any suggestions contained in this book, consult your physician or mental health professional. Neither the authors nor the publisher shall be liable or responsible for any loss or damage allegedly arising as a consequence of your use or application of any information or suggestions in this book.

Cover and text design: Miko Radcliffe at www.drawingacrowd.net.

Sacred Life Publishers™
www.SacredLife.com
Printed in the United States of America

In dedication to my dear husband,

Beto.

To other courageous souls who are

willing to experience dementia,

and to the loving caregivers in this world.

Contents

Introduction

This little book is a miracle to me, because all my life I was under the belief of not being able to put my thoughts into writing. It was part of my school experiences that produced a writer's block. I still can see some of my papers returned, filled with remarks written in red ink. When I would attempt to write a letter, I would get out the dictionary before the paper, being afraid of misspelling anything.

When we moved to Campbell, California, in 2009, I received a schedule of classes being offered at the Community Center, which included a Memoir Writing Class. The thought to overcome the inability of writing presented itself, and I enrolled, willing to give it a try.

The wonderful, gentle teacher explained to me what writer's block was, and then kindly guided me into my first attempts to tell some stories from my life. After sharing my very first memoir, she remarked, "You are a storyteller." She liked it, and I felt hope and joy.

It is never too late to overcome limitations!

That year I wrote more than I had written in over 60 years.

At a retreat with Neale Donald Walsch where I shared verbally some of my experiences with my "Immortal Beloved," our relationship, and the challenges of Alzheimer caregiving, I was encouraged to write about it. But I mentioned my fears of writing and being criticized. When Neale was helping me with his amazing insights, I suddenly saw my husband to my right, like a pop-up screen. With this came the message to write letters to him, for he loved me unconditionally, and the fear of being misunderstood dropped away. When I mentioned it to Neale, he smiled and said, "You just got your answer."

Divine Love inspires and leads the way in overcoming limitations.

Letters to My Immortal Beloved

My Dearest Beto, my Immortal Beloved, my Other Self!

These words we adopted from the first movie we saw together, *Immortal Beloved*, the story of Beethoven. When I saw your tears at the end of watching it, I knew I would love you forever.

We were blessed to meet so late in life; you were 68 years old and I was 15 years younger. However, our meeting was like seeing each other again from way back when, probably another lifetime.

It was at the potluck lunch with the "Conscious Connection" group in Santa Cruz, California, where we connected and never parted again. The leader of this association had told me about this friend of hers whose thinking was so much like mine that she wanted us to meet. Did she really know how much we thought alike? I doubt it, for I had no idea myself that two people could communicate in the way we did. That's why I called our relationship a *Communicationship*. After all, to relate and communicate are synonyms for me, and if the emphasis would be on *communicationship*, perhaps people would make sure that partners do that clearly. In your presence I experienced the absence of fear, complete freedom to be myself, which was new for me.

After the meal at the potluck lunch, there was Circle dancing. I couldn't wait for you to face me again and have us look into each other's eyes and sing, "May the Blessings of God rest upon you, may God's peace abide in you, may God's presence illuminate your heart, now and forever more."

We practiced this song many times again during our 17 years together but exchanged the word "God" with the synonym "Love," which was more meaningful to us--even until the end of your affliction with the dreadful disease. During those times we still gazed into each other's eyes and then embraced and cried together. That was something that the Alzheimer Monster could not take away from us.

After Circle dancing they played records of oldies from the sixties. We danced like children, free and without formalism.

We had fun!

When some members started to leave and I saw you putting on your shoes--we had been dancing in socks on a parquet floor--I dared to dash over to your corner, kick the second shoe away, and ask for another dance. I was stunned by my action, for in the past when

I liked a man, he would be the last one to find out about it. When the event was over, we went for a long walk on the beach and had lots of ideas to share. I told you about the speech I was preparing for Toastmasters, "The H M Computer."

At that time I was taking my first computer classes at a college, part of my retraining for another job after many years as a nurse. The things I learned there, I immediately related to the *Human Mind*, which is full of many programs and applications since birth, or before. We had a blast exploring more of that concept together, for we both had done a lot of work on our individual *Human Mind* computers in this lifetime.

Then we went to dinner at Dharma's, where I mentioned that I was healed of alcoholism through my studies of Christian Science. "Finally!" you exclaimed, "I meet someone healed of it instead of *recovering*."

At the resort where you lived at that time, we went in your hot tub and then, back at your cabin, we stood outside on a very narrow unfinished porch. The full moon was out, you took my hands and said, "It usually takes me a very long time before I get close to someone, but with you it's different. I feel like I'm in high school, and I would like to kiss you."

And we kisssssed.

Inside the cabin you read the following from your favorite book, *Emmanuel's Book II: The Choice for Love.*

The key to remembering
is to remind the self
not to be afraid of anything
anywhere
anytime
ever.

Illusion cannot destroy reality.
Can a shadow on the wall
hurt you?

Death cannot kill You.
Pain cannot hurt You.
Disease cannot make You ill.
Years cannot age You.
Fear cannot touch You.
Welcome Home.

Tears were rolling down my cheeks, and you were sniffling also. You had just read to me, in a nutshell, what I had studied for years as a student of metaphysics. We indeed were thinking alike.

We spent the night together with the under-standing of no sexual activity. For some reason, that did not fit in with our encounter. We talked and talked and embraced one another until past three o'clock. Again, it was a feeling of being reunited after a long time of separation.

This was our first day of heaven on earth together, and little did we know at that time what wonderful years were in store for us.

Mary Baker Eddy writes in her book, *Science and Health with Key to the Scriptures*, "Harmony in man is as real and as beautiful as in music." This always gave me great hope for the possibility of demonstrating and experiencing a harmonious relationship through the study and practice of the principle of Life and Love. Just like a musician, study and practice of the principal of music enables us to bring forth greater musical performances. Well, my dear, dear Hubby--the other day, when contemplating along those lines, it came to me in these words: "For 17 years we composed, practiced, and experienced a 'Grand Symphony of Love.'"

It was March 1995, when our first, glorious day together in heaven on earth happened. In November I was offered a new job, where I worked as an intern, in the Job Research Center. The manager of that place was going back to Ireland, and they thought I was qualified to take over. However, you and I wanted to take a vacation, since your massage school was closed in December and January. Wanting to be with you, I dared to ask them if I could start my duties on January

15th. "Well," my boss said, "If you get the counselors to cover for you those four weeks, it's fine with me." As you know, they did!

So off we went to spend four weeks of vacation in Baja California, Mexico. You had been there before, but for me, it was my first time in Mexico.

When we crossed the border and drove through Mexicali, I have to confess that I was quite scared. I was thinking, "Where in the world is he taking me?" But when we got out of the city, which didn't even have lanes on the streets at that time--and the traffic appeared to be rather chaotic--my heart slowed down, and I was able to enjoy the beautiful scenery of the desert and mountains.

Two hours later we entered San Felipe, and again I got concerned about my surroundings; but continuing further south it got interesting again, with more mountains to the west and the gorgeous blue Sea of Cortez to the east. As we drove south, I read the map and named all the Campos to you. Finally, you made a left turn into Campo El Vergel with the tall, white, light-tower.

We met a gentleman there who spoke English, an American, brown from the Baja sun. He took us to the owner, who showed us possible campsites. We settled for the one directly at the beach under a pine tree. When we asked about the price, "Whatever you think you can pay," was the answer. I think we paid $50 for four weeks.

You know, it took me a whole week to unwind and relax before enjoying our wonderful surroundings. At first I thought, "What in the world are we going to do here for four weeks!"

We found out quickly from other Americans about a Christmas dinner at the doctor's house, served by his wife. We got tickets for the event and joined quite a few *gringos* there. The interesting thing was that we had never seen that many happy people in one place, and they were very friendly and welcoming to us.

One of the couples, Less and Darlene, showed up the next day in their dune buggy, all bundled up in winter clothes while we were basking in the sun in our swimsuits. They were happy to find us there, for they had driven along the beach for over five miles to bring a flyer, which was an invitation to their New Year's Eve party. How sweet of them. We accepted the invitation and had a great time at their lovely round house, with panoramic views. It was a full house, and we met a lot of new people from all corners of the world. This couple inspired us to our eventual move to the region, and we often referred to them as our sponsors.

My Dear Beto,

When I was at our house alone recently, these dear friends came by after they heard about your passing. We embraced each other and cried together, missing you terribly. You probably were with us there, feeling our pain.

Back to our vacation: At that time I was struggling with some painful physical challenges that made my life in the workforce very difficult. One day at the beautiful beach where we had parked our camper, you (my dear, new friend) came back from an exploring walk with the exciting news that you had met a couple who was living there and were able to do that on $500.00 a month. "So," you said, "if we can find a place to live here, you will not have to work anymore, for my retirement income would be more than enough."

A rush of energy went through my body, and the thought of not having to drag myself to work--and being free--illuminated me with an incredible sense of joy. Adventure had always been a big driving force in my life. By selling my house in San Jose, California, we could build a place right there on the beach. What a possibility!

But wait! My independence had a voice also and did not want to have to rely on someone else for income. So I mentioned my concern and proposed to you that because the funds for the house we would be building came from the sale of my home, I would charge you rent so that I would have some income also. You agreed.

Close to our camping spot was a cement slab that we thought would be suitable for a home for us. We measured it and then designed a floor plan. We were sizzling with excitement.

The next day we walked around in the Campo and met some more people who had built houses there and had come for the New Year's celebration. We enthusiastically shared our plans with them, but their reaction was, "It would be a miracle to get an ocean-front lot here; there are others in line for the cement slab."

"Well," I said, "I believe in miracles."

Another homeowner joined us and invited us to see what he had done. As we entered his house, I experienced another energy rush. There in front of us was the floor plan we had designed the night before, completed as a house. Amazing!

After touring the home right at the Sea of Cortez, we went back to the camper. On our way there, you pulled out the business card of the owner of that lovely house and said, "He wants to sell his place." Oh my, what wonderful news!

Then, as you used to say, "**We rode the wave.**" In March you paid the down payment, in June I was able to sell my house, on the Fourth of July we drove back to Baja and bought it, and on September 23, 1996, we moved to our heavenly home on earth. It was my birthday when we arrived: That's why I remember that date so well--it was my best birthday gift ever.

Oh, and then our special bonus: A full, lunar eclipse right in front of the house. First was the rising of the moon out of the water, and next was watching the eclipse in full sight.

The night sky was often our awesome entertainment: lying in the hammock and counting the satellites go by. And then came the discovery that the strange bank of clouds every night in the same spot turned out to be the Milky Way. Boy, looking at that with our binoculars was absolutely spectacular.

You know, when living back here in the States and once in a while getting a glimpse of the moon or stars, I always felt a longing pain in my chest, missing our view of the night sky from our south deck in Baja. However, since my last visit to our house, it's not a home anymore. I came to the conclusion that I could not move back there and be by myself. So after that night of feeling terribly alone and, on top of it, having some physical challenges, I made the decision to turn it into a rental. I felt your approval, for I heard you saying, "You don't belong here anymore."

It was a good decision, for now when I get a little view of the moon once in a while, I am free of pain and longing. I feel a sense of peace instead.

While being there at our former home, we also followed your request to have your ashes spread in the Sea of Cortez, right there at the lovely beach in front of our house.

Emergency interruption: Today is January 3, 2013. It's a very challenging, sad day for me because our Nico cat passed over to where you are. It was horrible to see him getting sick so quickly. Perhaps you were with us all the way, but I need to let you know my side of the story.

I got up about three o'clock and he was lying on the floor in the hallway, breathing very shallow and fast. I got into panic mode, got dressed, scooped him up in my arms, and took him to the Emergency Clinic not far from here. After exams and x-rays, the doctor told me that Nico, Big boy, had an enlarged heart and his lungs were filled with fluid . . . and then some more. So I had to decide what to do with him--thousands of dollars of treatments and meds--or letting him join you. Well, since the thousands of dollars weren't at hand, his prolonged life here would have been only about two weeks to a few months, and with him being frightened of his own shadow, I had to let him go.

This part of life on earth sure sucks; it's the most painful process we have to go through, at least for me. I know, I know, you were ahead of me in that respect, but you also shed a tear when Rico, our other cat, was killed by a pack of dogs.

Now, our family here in our little apartment has been cut in half. You and Nico are there and Sissily and I are here. It isn't easy, for I miss you both terribly, even though I know that you are as close to me as my thoughts, spiritually speaking.

So I hope you and Nico are together happily, for I know he missed you here, and I feel he wanted to be united again with you. I picture him embraced in your arms.

Back to my reminiscing of our wonderful journey with you, our heaven on earth: Once our helping crew of the move to Baja left, we had lots to unpack and organize, and I remember it as very harmonious and joyful. We were not in a hurry, took time to go to the beach, and swim and sunbathe in between, knowing we had lots of time to get settled.

My cat, Wilbur, moved there with us. He had

adopted me 16 years prior to our move and had been my best friend. He was anxious to explore his new surroundings, and I invited him to go with me to the beach. You said, "He won't go close to the water," but he surprised you big time. First, when we went down the staircase, past the bushes, he saw the sand dune and it looked like he had found the biggest sandbox ever. So he used it and then followed me to the water. As soon as we got into the wet sand, however, he sat down and observed the shallow waves. He was a brave cat, but that was close enough.

Did I ever read to you the letter that I wrote to Wilbur after he transitioned? Well, here it is:

Dearest Wibby,

Today I was going to write *about* you for my memoir-writing class, but decided to write *to* you instead.

Among all the little friends I was privileged to have in this life, you are very special. Our beginning started in an unusual way. Whereas I adopted all the other buddies, you adopted me. When you came to my back door, fully grown, and wanting to come in, I would gently push you out with my foot and tell you to go home, assuming that you had one. You then would look right at me with your piercing eyes and give me the message, "But I know you love cats!"

"Yes, that's true, but I have two cats already," I would reply.

This became a regular encounter for several days until you reminded me of the **book,** *Kinship with All Life,* and remarked, "If you really understood what's in that book, you would treat me differently and take me in." Realizing that you were absolutely right, I took you into my arms for the first time and welcomed you to our family.

Someone came up with the name of "Wilbur," which stuck with you even though I did not like it very much. So I called you Wibby instead. Later on, however, I thought you needed a middle name that would sound just right; so you became Wilbur Alexander Paul, sounding like Russian royalty in my opinion.

Shortly after your arrival, our family fell apart, and Daniel (twelve years old at that time), three cats, and I remained in our home. It was a very challenging time, as you probably remember, for you became a big support to me. One day when standing in the living room leaning against the wall and crying my little eyes out, you instantly appeared at my side, got on your hind feet, put your front paws on my leg, and licked my hand. Another day when crying in bed at night you repeated that sweet gesture and let me know that you would not leave me comfortless.

You were right! The next 17 years you stayed with me as my best friend. Daniel grew up and left home, and the other two buddy cats finished their lives early.

At one time I had a job as a private nurse for an elderly gentleman in Marin County. You were welcome there also and would commute with me in the car. After a few trips you wanted to travel out of the cage and surprised me how well you could do that. You would stand on the back seat, your front paws on the top of the front seat, and watch the world go by. It always reminded me of *Puss in Boots*, a movie I saw as a youngster.

Our next home was a brand new condo in San Jose. I was told to keep you indoors for at least two weeks. You, however, did not agree with that and rushed outside on the second morning before I could catch you. So I followed in my robe and caught up with you in one of the unfinished houses you started to investigate. When a man appeared to see what I was doing there, you shot right by us like an arrow, straight back into our new home. "I think that was a cat," the man remarked. So I explained to him why I was out there in my robe. Fortunately the fences had not been built at that time. From that day on, you were free to come and go as you wished.

Since we did not have a cat door like in the old home, you had to let me know somehow when you wanted to get back in. You were amazing in knowing what room I would be in, for you always went to the window of that room to *miau miau.* (German cat talk.)

Another mind-boggling event was at the facility where I worked in a group home. Since I had to stay there five days a week, I had my own room, and you stayed with me. The first time I let you outside, you went to the other side of the seven to eight foot chain-link fence and threw me into panic. "How in the world did you get up there, and how am I going to get you back!" You gave me a very strange look, started running towards the fence, jumped (touching the chain links with precision), flew over the top, and landed on the inside as gracefully as only a cat can. Then giving me another interesting look, as if to say, "Now you know how I can do all these things," you marched straight to the door to be let in.

Morning meditations we loved to do together. I will never forget the one morning when you intensely looked into my eyes and mentally told me, "When you meet your soul mate, I am free to go."

"No way. There will be room for all of us."

Well, I guess you knew the future, for I met my soul mate a year later, and when we moved to Baja, Mexico, you came with us for the first year. After returning to San Jose the following summer, you got very sick, had a hard time breathing, and the doctor said that you probably would not survive an x-ray. So I had to let you go.

When leaving the doctor's office I could not stop crying, and on the way home I thought, "I wish I had held him a little longer and said goodbye more intensely."

In that moment of despair you again comforted me; you let me feel your presence and said, "I haven't gone anywhere. I am right here." Then you showed me the different levels of consciousness, the one missing your body and weeping--and the one communicating on a spiritual level. Both were fine, neither right nor wrong, or one better than the other, just different, for me to choose. Wow, what an insight!

A year later, when packing for the summer to go to California, I suddenly started crying again, missing you so very much. On the way to Ensenada I mentally reached out to you and asked for some clarification on this spiritual communication stuff. You were right away present again and gave me the most wonderful message, "I am a Being that is always with you, and for a time I took on the form of a cat, to be physically close to you in this lifetime." Then you let me see something that is beyond words. It is also beyond words how grateful I am for your love, dearest Wilbur Alexander Paul!

Lovingly,
Your Petmom

Dearest Beto,

Little did I know then how that dear friend Wilbur would be again a comforter and teacher in the future, when the Alzheimer Monster tried to destroy our *communicationship*. But more later about that.

However, I must tell you about an interesting story from last summer. I was visiting our friend Susanna's place, who was on a trip for a few days, and on my way from the swimming pool to her apartment, a cat looking exactly like Wilbur was coming towards me. He looked at me, strolled around my legs, and behaved just like my old friend. I picked him up and snuggled with him, and of course my tears were rolling. We visited for a while, and then he followed me just like in old times. A gentleman watching us asked if it was my cat. "No," I said, "but he looks exactly like a cat I used to have." Well, after some more petting I told my new, old friend that he needed to stay behind, close to his new home. So he sat down and watched me go away.

After Susanna came home, we both went for a swim, and on the way back, I called, "Wibby, where are you?" He promptly appeared from the bushes to the left, looking like he'd just finished a nap--stretching and again greeting me the same way like the first encounter.

A couple of weeks later when visiting Susanna again, he was in the back parking lot. I called him and he came running to me immediately, so I picked him up to embrace him again. Then I noticed nearby a woman with a dog watching me. When I asked her if this was her cat she nodded. So I told her that he looked just like my cat that was my best friend for 17 years. She was quite moved by my story for she had tears in her eyes also.

My take on this was that Wibby showed up again to comfort me at a time of struggle.

But now back to our life in Campo El Vergel, our heaven on earth.

At summer times we needed to pack up and go north, for the heat and humidity was too much for us. The first summer we stayed with our friends Susanna and Pablo and also did some house sitting for my son **Daniel.** During the house sitting, something happened to my back, and you, Dear One, took me to the emergency room. The outcome of that resulted in two surgeries during which you, Gentle Beam of Love and Life, became the best caregiver I have ever encountered. You not only took care of me, you also were my coach, encouraging me to exercise and take walks (with you at my side). All that and more with the greatest, gentle presence that you are. You never seemed to display any impatience or tiredness; instead you presented cheerfulness, joy, encouragement, and any other loving quality one can think of. Words can never express my deepest gratitude to you for your support during those weeks.

Our friends Susanna and Pablo also stood by me during that time. They let us stay at their place until I was well enough to go home again.

They also were the first ones to visit us at the Sea of Cortez. The four of us surely were a wonderful bunch, so laid back and not demanding, as well as respecting each other's space, likes, and dislikes. That's probably why they became our frequent visitors over the years and brought much joy into our lives. They surely fit into our circle of harmony.

Pablo liked to explore the desert, and we went on several off-road trips together. One year after the region had been blessed with lots of rain and the desert was beautifully in full bloom, Pablo dug up one of the lilies and planted it next to our garage. Other people had told us that they won't grow again, but this one reappeared twice after some rain, and it bloomed. I called it our Miracle Lily. And guess what! On my latest trip there during February and March, that precious lily bloomed for me again.

Miracle Lily

You and Pablo surely had fun with the solar panels and electrical system. Our garage and roof became his lab for the idea of a rotating solar panel setup. The two of you spent many hours on the roof and looked very happy.

Sadly for us, Pablo made his transition two and a half years before you, three months before his retirement. We all were shocked and missed him a lot.

Now, however, the two of you are probably quite happy, sharing again Beingness wherever you are.

Susanna and I are a great support to each other in our trying times of missing you both. We are exploring all kind of ways to connect with you, will tell you later about it. But I am getting ahead of myself here.

So back to our activities in Baja.

After settling in, we got involved with a reading group in San Felipe. The first book they were reading when we joined was Eckhardt Tolle's *The Power of Now*. Great discussions followed, and we made some very dear friends. Other books that followed were *Conversations with God*, by Neale Donald Walsch, *The Four Agreements*, by Don Miguel **Ruiz, and more.**

We got much inspiration in those get-togethers with **like-minded** friends.

One year, we and some of our new friends went on a long tour to the south of Baja, which included a whale watching event--the highlight of the trip. This is the bay where the gray whales have their babies.

We boarded a *panga* (a little boat) early in the morning, when the water was as smooth as glass. Dolphins were swimming alongside right away, and in the distance we saw some whales mounting out of the water. Apparently the whales are familiar with the boats, for they come close to be touched. After I stroked one of the mothers she turned slightly on her side so her eye could see us more clearly (I guess). Then our eyes met for a few seconds, and I felt an incredible surge of love. It surely was an awesome feeling to have that encounter with such a large animal.

Back at home we often brought some books onto the front deck in the mornings, watching the sunrise, meditating, and reading to each other. It happened sometimes that we opened the books randomly and found the same ideas presented with different vocabulary. We practiced our *communicationship*!

One of the early insights of good communication you gave to me was the way you let me know when something bothered you. Let's say, for instance, a habit of mine or a behavior from my childhood programming made you feel uncomfortable. You would approach me at a leisure time with these words, "I have a request," and then you would very gently explain to me what you disliked and ask me how and if we could work on this, so we both can benefit from the change.

The first time you did that, I was in awe, for in my other two marriages these feelings were suppressed, and years later those suppressed feelings brought forth anger and resentment. So, of course, I would do anything to do something about my habits or shortcomings, to maintain harmony and joy. "Should I slip in my endeavor to let go of it, please help me to stay on target," I would throw in as a safety precaution, which you always accomplished ever so gently.

Recently, I shared this with a friend who had experienced failed marriages, and he replied with the story that he did not like it when his wife cluttered the dining table with her art stuff. So he built her a nice large table in the garage, which she gratefully received. After a short time the dining table was cluttered again, so he built her another provision in the bedroom. But that did not solve his problem either. Now he could see, and smiled about it, that he could have communicated his dislike in a much easier manner.

Another little incident I remember so fondly is the answer you gave me after I referred to you as my husband, long before we got married. When you looked at me, startled, I made a remark about a Freudian slip and then shared with you the definition of that word, which I--your new friend the word-looker-upper--had found in her much used dictionary. "Promoter of growth" it is. "Oh," you replied, "Then you are my husband also!" Yes, my sweet promoter of growth, our expansion of consciousness in the years we were privileged to spend together was quite a jump of growth, even though we both had progressed a lot in this lifetime before we met.

Remember my experience and "Aha" moment on top of Mount Tamalpais, north of San Francisco, which gave me some help with my concept of relation/*communicationship*.

A coworker and I, at a private school, had taken a ditch day, something that was "in" and a custom at the private school where we worked. We had chosen the top of the mountain as our outing and were sitting there in the sun at the very edge of a beautiful vista point, reading to each other. There were several birds soaring at that altitude, and I was admiring them. Out of the corner of my eye I spotted some franticly fluttering birds on the side of the mountain right above the bushes. "Silly birds," I thought, "Why don't you join the soaring ones?" When focusing closer, I saw that they were not birds at all, they were the shadows of the birds above. Instantly a quote **from one of Mary Baker Eddy's hymns** presented itself, "By flesh **embound** was but thy shade." Hmm, I reasoned, the shadows, bodies, of individuals can be close together, even though the real Beings can be at very different altitudes of consciousness. But in order to experience a "communication," one has to be soaring closely together. You confirmed that concept, after I shared it with you, by telling me about reading in a book a long time ago that, if you are more than three levels apart, only talking happens but not true communicating. This was another instant of rejoicing for us, to discover our mutual viewpoints.

Our openness for learning and letting go of pre-conceived ideas was wonderful. When you found out that I had studied Christian Science you were at first concerned and voiced your concepts of it. "So you are not allowed to go to a doctor or take medicine." That was a quote I heard often from misinformed individuals. Over the years, however, you were amazed how false those statements are. Just the opposite is true, for in the textbook, *Science and Health with Key to the Scriptures*, by Mary Baker Eddy, her students are encouraged to get other help if they cannot heal themselves readily. On page **443** she writes,

> If patients fail to experience the healing power of Christian Science, and think they can be benefited by certain ordinary physical methods of medical treatment, then the Mind-physician should give up such cases, and leave invalids free to resort to whatever other systems they fancy will afford relief.

And on page **401,**

> Until the advancing age admits the efficacy and supremacy of Mind, it is better for Christian Scientists to leave surgery and the adjustment of broken bones and dislocations to the fingers of a surgeon, while the mental healer confines himself chiefly to mental reconstruction and to the prevention of inflammation.

We both were quite sensitive about prejudice and I thought you might like what I wrote about it in the memoir-writing class:

A Closer Look at Prejudice

The taste of being discriminated against or prejudged was introduced to me in early childhood. We were refugees after WWII and the locals looked down on us.

When I was in the eighth grade, our family moved to a city that was predominately catholic, and I had to go to a catholic school. In a class of about twenty students, there were four of us protestant, and the teachers treated us accordingly.

In my early time in New York (and still today here in the USA), I was called many names as a German.

In a true story my grandmother told me about her experience in WWI, she taught me not to discriminate against Russians: When soldiers came to her house, they showed their gentle side by being moved by a crying baby (my mother), and consequently left without taking anything.

As an employee in a private **high school**, I was asked by the history teacher to tell his class about my family's experience during WWII. After finishing my story one of the students commented. "I did not know that the Germans suffered."

My family's story was mild in comparison to others. We had a neighbor who did not get out before the Russian army marched in. She told horror stories how the women were raped and then had their bellies cut open. When she saw them lying at the side of the street, she held her hands over her belly and ran and ran and ran until she could not run anymore and was able to get out of the situation. A nurse I worked with who was a teenager during that time told me how she still had nightmares about her family's mistreatment by the Russian soldiers. Her father got decapitated, and the family had to walk by the **head** and greet him.

When I heard the **high school** student utter his ignorance I felt that he got his information from *Hogan's Heroes*, a TV series from WWII.

Ignorance is a producer of prejudice. But wait, propaganda is needed in the production also; they are joined at the hip.

In my case, concerning Russians, my grand-mother's influence was stronger than the horror stories, plus the understanding that soldiers who have lived through dreadful war times can become monsters. This helped me to understand that not all Russians are bad.

Recently, on our walks in the park near our home, we have met Russian senior citizens and have become friends with them. They are some of the most precious people I have met in my life.

Having lived in Baja for fourteen years, I have come to respect the culture of Mexico. To me the core of the Mexicans are people with big hearts, full of love. And yet I have heard many negative remarks about them. Sure, there are banditos, but they can be found in any country. It is sad to me how some people talk about illegal immigrants. After reading a little book about them risking their lives to get to the U.S.A., how they are ripped off of their meager possessions, sometimes killed, and then sent back to Mexico to live like rats in a garbage dump in Tijuana, one gets a very different view of them.

Writing about garbage brings back to mind an experience I had about twenty years ago. On my daily walk to a park, I had to pass a bus stop that was cluttered with leftovers from local fast food restaurants, with lots of paper wrappings and little boxes, etc. The thought had come many times to bring a plastic bag and clean up the place, since I was unemployed at the time and should do something good for the community. My resistance to that task was strong, for it was dirty stuff. One day somebody had added a large, black plastic bag to the heap, and it looked like it was placed there for me to fill. But I passed by.

The following day an empty shopping cart was placed next to the messy scene, and when passing by again with my two bags of old bread for the ducks in the park, the thought was even stronger to do the cleanup job. After feeding the ducks and almost throwing the bags into the trash, the little voice suggested putting them over my hands and that way my little clean hands would not be touching the stuff. "Okay," I answered to the little voice, and on my way back I took the time to fill that big, black plastic bag with all that clutter, putting it into the shopping cart and marching towards the shopping center where I knew there was a big trash can. On the way there it started to sprinkle, and I felt everybody passing by in their cars giving me a certain look with the remark, "There goes another bag lady."

At my arrival at the shopping center just before the deposit of the big bag into the bigger trash can, a lady was coming from the drugstore toward me, and when seeing me, she let out a strange sound and made a big circle around me. Little did she know about my story by looking at the appearance.

With all that knowledge about prejudice, one could get the idea that I am free of it. Oh no! I, also, have been influenced by propaganda of some sort or another. After all, I, like most, do watch TV.

Recently when enjoying a new DVD of a concert by

Andre Rieu in South Africa, he announced at one point that the next song to be performed would be by the late, great musician Michael Jackson and would be played in his honor and commemoration. My reaction was fierce: "Not him!" My mind was screaming within, and a picture of him holding a little child off a balcony flared up, along with so many cosmetic surgeries. That's all I knew of Michael from TV propaganda, and I had formed a negative picture of him. Little did I know what was in store for me. The song, *Heal the World*, which I had never heard before, was absolutely awesome. I went online to get the lyrics, and they gave me an insight of his true Being, the Being behind the mask, **that was yearning to heal the world with love.**

Thank you, Michael Jackson, for that wonderful gift to me and humanity, and please forgive me for forming such a false concept of you out of ignorance and propaganda. Your beautiful song is now in my heart with a true concept of you, and I sing it often.

Dearest Soul Mate,

One day, my love, you started to change. At first I thought that it was a mini-stroke you encountered, but three years later you were diagnosed with Alzheimer's disease. I was in denial for quite a while and even distanced myself from you because of this changed behavior. When I visited an Alzheimer's Association office, the very kind and friendly people there gave me a package of literature, which included a book that was written by a coach whose wife was afflicted with that dreadful disease. This book helped me a lot. I remember clearly when I read the words, "This is the time when they need more love than ever before." That sentence awakened me out of my denial, and I realized the horrible frustration you were experiencing. An overwhelming feeling of love and compassion overcame my whole being. I wept and wept; I felt sad that I had not been a better support because of my denial and ignorance.

Oh, the lessons I had to learn the following years. The first lesson was patience, the second was not to take anything personally. The third was when strange behavior was presented I was not dealing with you, my dearest husband, but rather I was confronted with Alzheimer's disease, the monster.

The first thing that was taken away from your memory was the remembrance of operating **mechanical** tasks, a very important aspect of our life in the desert of Baja. So the time came when we had to leave our precious home, our heaven on earth.

Our friend Pablo was the administrator of a senior housing complex in Campbell, California. And he was able to provide a studio apartment for us. I remember how devastated I felt when I packed our car with the most necessary things, for I knew we probably could not come back to our home. And so it was. We spent one year in that little apartment before we were able to move into a one-bedroom place.

I was told by many dear friends to look for support, which I finally did. I was led to many wonderful support groups, and the doctors at the VA hospital were also very helpful during my journey through the disease.

A big shift in my consciousness took place one morning when I was quite devastated and I mentally reached out for help. My good, old, cat-buddy "Wilbur" came to me through my thoughts, and it was as **if he was talking to me. "Remember when you had to let me go and you wished** you would have held me a little longer and said goodbye more intensely?"

"Yes," I replied. "I do remember".

"Well, now you have the opportunity to do this with your dear husband!" Oh my, what a message, what a gift.

I followed his advice, and I knew when I consciously held you, my Immortal Beloved, my other Self—when I held you a little longer and mentally said more intensely goodbye--we both could feel the unspeakable love that we always have for each other.

Another great gift I received was through a DVD for Alzheimer's caregivers, which a dear lady at the daytime activity center had given me after I asked her for help in caring for you. In this DVD, they pointed out that the most important thing in my caring was to make you, the patient, feel better about yourself. What important advise! After thinking about this for a while, the question arose, "Why wait for someone to have a dreadful disease to practice this? Wouldn't relation-ships work out better in general if our priority would be to make another person feel better about him or herself? Or if we would treat ourselves in this way, we would feel better about ourselves, and we could change the world."

Since I liked this DVD so much, I wanted to buy one for myself and for some relatives and friends because I felt anyone can benefit from the information on it. So I went online and was surprised that it was rather expensive: over $100. I felt impelled to call the number anyway and to let them know how much I appreciated their work. When I asked the lady answering the phone, "Who produced this DVD?" She said, "I did."

"Oh, then I can thank you personally and tell you how much help I received from your instructions." She was very happy to get some feedback, for generally this DVD goes to institutions for training purposes and they don't give much feedback. She also had the experience of dealing with Alzheimer's disease of a loved one and agreed with me that we learn a lot in this process and become more patient and compassionate. We talked for quite a while and when I mentioned to her the high price of the DVD she replied that I would be able to get it for less. However, after a very inspiring communication, she asked for my address and how many I needed. "Four," was my answer.

Then this kind lady said, "I am going to send you four copies plus the newest DVD for advanced stages of the disease as a gift." I was stunned and tears of gratitude were rolling.

Even though I was learning many things spiritually as well as humanly, I have to confess that there were occasions when I let the monster disease disturb our harmony. As much as I knew how frustrating the experience was for you, I did fail a few times to keep my cool and got angry, even yelling at you. Especially one time when you got up from the breakfast table and the breakfast stuff you had lined up at the edge of the table all fell down, including a full carton of milk. Being totally upset about it, you let the milk carton have it and stomped with gusto on it so the milk splashed in all directions. There was a knee-jerk reaction in me, and I would like to apologize for the angry language that came out of my mouth.

You see, if something like that would happen right now, I would consciously stop and choose a different response, perhaps even laugh about it. Because now I am more able to make conscious choices, and it does not make a difference that something like that has to be cleaned up, either with anger or with a sense of humor.

Then the two 911 calls that I had to make within a couple of weeks when the Alzheimer Monster screamed louder than ever before: that almost crushed me to pieces. You were taken to the emergency room at the VA hospital, where you received medication, and the monster disease calmed down.

At the second 911 call, the same firemen came again, and the one kind officer took me aside and admonished me to let you go, for a combative patient could endanger my life; and then I could be of no more help. The physicians at the VA hospital gave the same advice to me.

This was a very, very, hard decision to make, which I was not able to do during the first hospital stay. And even though a kind social worker had planned how to get you into a care facility, I was so devastated that I almost thought I would go nuts. So I took you home with me instead. But the second time you were on another unit, and the social worker there found a place we could afford. **Nevertheless, bringing you there and leaving you behind in that facility, again, was a very trying time for me. Thank God that Daniel was able to be with us at that time, for he was a big support.**

After you settled in, I was able to visit and even take you out to your favorite restaurants, especially the Dairy Queen for ice cream. My visits became quality times for us, and we both enjoyed them.

Your ability to speak also diminished over the years. I could feel your frustration and learned to guess what you wanted to tell me. After we went to see the movie *The King's Speech*, I will never forget how you emphatically said, "I know exactly how he felt!" Oh yes, and I knew how you, my dear husband, felt when you could not get out the words you wanted to say. As the illness progressed, I realized that in your frustration you started to give up. You would start a sentence and then say, "Forget it, never mind." It was so hard to witness this and I felt so helpless. It actually got to the point that you got angry when I wanted to help you. It was just too much to deal with, so I started to give up also. Humanly, that is, but with a little metaphysical understanding I started addressing you mentally; and lo and behold, you responded.

It is often said that older people with dementia are like little children, but that is not true; for being treated and taught like a child would trigger anger and frustration in them. That's robbing them of their dignity. You surely were sensitive to that. On that note, I received a big help from an interview we watched with Jill Bolte, a brain scientist, who suffered a major bleeding in her brain, recovered over a period of seven to eight years, and wrote the book, *My Stroke of Insight*. She described how her caregivers treated her, and the most important thing I learned from that interview is her quote, "We are not stupid, we are wounded."

Right now, **another** friend comes to mind. Remember how he got upset when he heard that you were on the beta blocker, Atenolol? He told us that he had been taking it and found out very quickly that it affected his mind in a very negative way. So he advised us to ask your doctor for another blood pressure medication, which we did; and after you were off that stuff you got so much better. Even your neurologist remembered me reporting to her, "I got my husband back." Yes, I got you back for a while, and I am convinced that because one of the side effects of Atenolol is short-term memory loss, it did something to your brain. Probably a lot of other patients also had bad side effects from that drug. But can you imagine the pharmaceutical and medical industry ever admitting such an error? They would be zapped by the law industry big time. Who knows, perhaps the terrible increase of that dreadful disease is linked to that and other meds.

Take our friend's experience for instance, who got so ill with Alzheimer's and other ailments that she ended up in a nursing home. Fortunately, the staff there took all her meds away and started over with those she really needed. Lo and behold, she got well and was able to join her husband at home again. We saw her again at a fire station fundraiser fiesta and she looked and acted great. What a joy to have her back!

Hi, My Dear Beto,

The new year of 2013 has not started too great. First was Nico leaving me, and then on the eighth I got sad news about a friend's son having departed also. Daniel and I went to the funeral to be of comfort to those in tragic distress.

Now after some resting I want to snuggle up with you mentally by writing and letting you know that all the trials that the AM, Alzheimer Monster, and your departure have taught me were of great help and gave me strength in being able to have far greater compassion and understanding of those dear ones being in shock and grief.

The interesting thing was that I had made an appointment prior with a medium, which turned out to be two hours before the funeral. So I got a clearer view of the whole happening and the assurance that the young boy was happy and well cared for. It is a great comfort to me to dive into the spirit dimension, and I am eager to learn more how to connect with you and others who have gone before.

I went with some of our reading group members to San Francisco today to listen to a lecture by Deepak

Chopra. It was very inspiring to hear him talk about science coming closer to spirituality. Remember how I told you about reading in a book by the same author of *Kinship with All Life*, that "The common belief is that we are in the body, but the opposite is true, namely, that the body is in us," and how much impact that had on me? That was many years ago, and today it was told to hundreds of people in the grand ballroom at the Hyatt Regency Hotel. What a wonderful blessing **Deepak Chopra** is to humanity!

Today was on the gloomy side. A wonderful counselor who helped me with my sadness after you passed over, explained to me how grief works. "It comes in waves, so just go with the wave, and over time they will not be as high and will be less frequent." She was right, I do have less tears and not as often, but today they came full blast. **Yes, I know, they came, to pass. It is interesting how t**he little things we used to do together will trigger a wave.

A friend of mine, who lost her husband also, calls them land mines. They blow us up at the strangest places and times. I did the laundry today and remembered how we worked like a team with those chores. So I missed you big time, especially when putting the duvet cover over the comforter--I could picture your dear hands holding tightly onto the corners while I pulled the cover over the rest of it. Oh my dear one, it's still hard at times, even though I know that you are free now and happy. Without the help I received from working with mediums and taking workshops, I do not know how I would have survived without spiritual support.

Other land mines I have encountered happen while shopping. I see Reese's **Peanut Butter Cups** on sale and start to tear up because I cannot buy them anymore for you--or sweet potatoes or Tapioca pudding and many other things. But even those tear-jerkers are getting less as time goes by.

Let me tell you about some of my saving "Angels." In one of the first caregiver support groups I attended, I met one of them. Angels, that is. When I told her in tears that I had to let you go to a nursing home and how horrible that was for me having been a nurse all my life, she actually started to tear up also, feeling my pain. She was very comforting and told me about a program at a hospital nearby, "Older Adults Transitional Services," OATS in short. That program saved me from joining the high percentage of caregivers that pass on before the Alzheimer's patient. Yes, you read correctly: caregivers are killed by the Alzheimer Monster! Little did I know how deep I had fallen into depression. Actually, I had no knowledge of what depression is.

For fifteen weeks I attended the teaching and therapy sessions of that wonderful gift for four days each week. The counselors and teachers are more of my Angels. Their patience, love, expertise, and encouragement pulled me back into life. My gratitude to them is beyond words.

One insight that I shared with them, which had helped me, was an interesting concept I received one morning in Baja while meditating at sunrise on our front porch. The concept of our body being a tool came to mind, and I asked what kind of tool it was. "A living microscope you put on planet Earth," came the answer.

"Sort of like Rover on Mars?"

"No." with a giggle, "A little more sophisticated, for zooming in and out."

You see, I had zoomed in on the Alzheimer Monster, got so overwhelmed and almost hypnotized, that I forgot to zoom out. I had allowed it to take over my life, our lives, and lost interest in anything else. So during those weeks at OATS I remembered to zoom out again. This happened when they showed a drawing and explained that the Alzheimer Monster is "part" of my life at this time. Yes, it's sad and terrible and will probably be there for a long time, but I had to look and open up to a much larger picture of my life. They can coexist if I let them do just that.

Before that, my life was consumed with **caregiving;** now I was learning to put it in its proper place, open up, and let the sunshine in again.

During that time, some members of our reading group invited me to their church, Center for Spiritual Living. I accepted this one Sunday and went for a visit. After parking my car and going towards the entrance, I saw a couple just leaving from the earlier service. It took me a few moments to recognize our old-time friends Peter and Joyce, neighbors of yours a long time ago. We embraced and I pretty much broke down while telling them why you were not with me. Our friends told me that they had been searching for us the last two years without success. This assured me that I was in the right place at the right time.

A lady, Michelle, being concerned about me, brought me a glass of water and showed much compassion. As it turned out, she was the head of the choir in the music department. A few weeks later I was singing with them. She is a great spiritual practitioner, and it is amazing how she directs the rehearsals. She sees us as the presence of God and knows we can sing it all correctly. We are good friends now, and she had someone compose and then perform a special composition of the cannon *Dona Nobis Pacem* and *All is Well,* just for you and me. Boy, was that a beautiful, heartwarming surprise! What a gift! You see, on the day you moved into the Hospice Unit, I went to choir practice in the evening, and she was led to form a circle, and we sang "All is well, all shall be well, all manner of things shall be well." Oh, what a comfort that was to my soul!

The Monday after my first visit to the Center for Spiritual Living, on my way to the OATS program, I found myself happy, ready to share with my group there. However, as soon as I became conscious of the joy, I felt guilty, since the Alzheimer Monster had attacked you, my dear husband, and that was sad. So how could I dare be happy at a time like this? While sharing with the counselors, I learned that we can be both at the same time. This caused a big shift in my thinking and has been very helpful in my way upward.

Another obstacle, though, came along to throw me for a loop. The home where you were being cared for sent me a 30-day notice that they could not care for you anymore. In my opinion, they did not have sufficient trained personnel to deal with the Alzheimer Monster. This catapulted me to the darkest hour of that time, for I could not find any other facility that we could afford; and the State institutions I had visited were so depressing that I could never have put you in one of those. Then there was one very nice place that was willing to take you for the same amount as the old one, and wait for the VA benefits to come through and get paid later--if and only if--the nurse (after meeting you) would give her okay. They had two Alzheimer units with trained nurses. I was to bring you there for a visit on a Monday before they made a decision.

The weekend before that my little mind went topsy-turvy. "What if they won't take him? You can't do it anymore . . ." **Then I remembered the Hollywood version of Alzheimer's in the movie *The Notebook* where, at the end, the couple were found together in bed and they had both passed away.**

That picture became stronger in my mind, and then the knowledge that in Europe there are pills available to end your life if you are terminally ill . . . . So the temptation to kill us all: you, the cats, and myself grew horribly out of proportion in my disturbed, frightened head. That night was the darkest time of my life. But my son and I had made a long-pledged promise between us that we never would commit suicide, for we know that it would be a horrible experience for the one staying behind. This feeling rose up from deep inside my memory bank.

Even though still being very much distraught Sunday morning, I had enough sense in me to go to the Center for Spiritual Living, found Rev. Susan, and stood there like an idiot telling her my horror story. She immediately got a practitioner; and thank God our friend Mark from the reading group was there, who took me by the hand and sat next to me during the service. When I talked to the practitioner afterward, he prayed with me and calmed my oh-so-troubled mind. I do not remember anything else from that day, but the next morning I was in a class at the Center and shared some of my dilemma. Wow, did people get busy, connecting with other Centers in California to start a prayer chain or whatever it is called. The next thing that happened was my friends Deanna and Mary came with me to pick you up and, I swear, on our way I felt so uplifted by that powerful prayer that I thought I was a few inches above my car seat.

You were happy to see us and delighted to be going with us, not knowing the new plans for you. At the San Carlos Elms you were very cordial, paid compliments to the **administrator** and staff, and were happy to receive brownies and cookies. While the nurse observed you, we filled out a ton of paperwork. You were the precious you, overriding the monster, and everybody loved you and decided to admit you right then and there.

Then we took you to the Alzheimer's unit and the nurse showed you to your room. That changed something in you, and you realized what was going on. You came towards me, took my hands, looked straight into my eyes and said, "You mean we will never have again what we used to have?"

You were perfectly normal in that moment, and I broke into tears and had to tell you, "No," and while I held you in my arms, I continued, "I am too sick, I cannot care for you anymore." Oh, how I wished I could have taken you home with me at that moment! We know now that Alzheimer patients cross over and come back many times, and at that moment you were with me totally.

You were happy there, and the staff was ever so kind and loving. When I visited, you were always happy to see me, and we had quality times together. The infection you got soon after you moved there, unfortunately, required returning to the VA Hospital, where you left your body permanently two and a half weeks later. During that time I hope you did not have to suffer or be in pain. You always knew me when I came to visit, and even though your speech was so limited, you still used your hand to give me the "I love you" sign, even the day before you passed over.

Shortly before you passed over, I was longing so very much to communicate with you, and the idea came to call the medium that Susanna had told me about. Her daughter had received much help from her, since she connects with animals, unborn babies, and infants. I called her and told her about us and that the Alzheimer's disease had made it almost impossible for you to talk.

"Well, I have never done that before, but I am willing to give it a try," was the answer. We made an appointment for a reading, and it worked! You responded.

The first observation she shared was, "His family is waiting for him, and somebody is stroking his hand, looks like a brother. Did one of his brothers pass over recently?"

"Yes," I replied, "Two months ago."

"He is comforting him."

"Now he says that he has a hard time making up his mind to cross over. Because he loves you so much, he does not want to let go."

"Tell him that I do not want him to suffer any longer, I am willing to let go and let him be free."

"He says that you told him that already."

"Yes, I did, but I did not know that he understood my message."

"He is afraid that you will forget him."

"Why would you think that? That is not possible."

Then the clarification was made that the Alzheimer years would overshadow the heavenly years. So the following day at your bedside on the hospice unit, I gently but firmly let you know that I was very clear that you and the disease were separate, that our true Beingness was the only reality and that was forever in our memory. Our years of heaven on earth could not be pushed aside by the appearance of a dreadful illness. The day after that you felt free to go. It was hard, but I survived.

Because of that conversation with the medium, I bought a multi-picture frame contraption and filled it with some of our happiest photos. They are a daily uplift for me.

Our Happiest Photos

Let me mention here how blessed I have been with meeting people who have had to care for someone with dementia, for they all have shown me the greatest compassion, understanding, and loving kindness. They all are impelled now to help others who are going through this trying experience.

Having cared for you, my beloved, this illness has certainly produced shifts in my thinking about many things, including the disease itself. In spite of gradually slipping into a deep depression and remembering those years as the most difficult of my life, I now can see the tremendous growth in myself that I would not have experienced without living through it. So, perhaps this dreadful disease is aiding humanity to evolve into a more caring and compassionate consciousness.

My Dear Loving Beto,

In November Daniel and I made a trip to Baja, to look after the house and to fulfill your request to have your ashes spread in the sea. Your son and wife joined us a week later to be part of that. They also took Daniel back to the States.

They left early in the morning, and I was left alone in the house that was once our home, our heaven on **earth.** It felt so empty, so cold, and the tears were rolling. So I had to decide how to experience the day: sad, missing you, or communicating with you on the spiritual level. Well, I did both. Up and down jumped my emotions, and I let them flow. I remembered a cloth calendar from many years ago that a friend had given me, with the words, "A house is just a dwelling place, God's love makes it a home." Divine Love surely was expressed by you, my dear husband, and by me in our happy days here. Yes, yes, I know God's love is ever present and not limited to a person, but that level of consciousness was not the one I was focusing on. I missed you terribly. Since there was much to do around the house and the workers were finishing up the roof replacement, I tried to shift the focus on that and got a few things done myself. When my dear helpers finished up at noon and left also, more waves of sadness rolled in. When talking with Josefina later on and apologizing for my behavior, she was so kind and supporting, "*Este natural*," she assured me.

Yes, I am in a house, a shell, that needs much improvement. What can I do while being here? I have some ideas, but the energy to do something is low, so I clean here a little, there a little, measure the windows and doors for future curtains, but it isn't fun. Plus, all the unexpected repairs put a big hole in the account. Why do it now, since I have to wait anyway for the back pay from the VA.

I spent most of Thursday with Marina in San Felipe. She needed to shop for her restaurant this weekend. She gets her meat at a special place in a part of town I had never visited and, lo and behold, it was Philipe, the owner of my favorite *Mercado* which had closed. What a joy to see him! He had been through rough times and has a very small shop now. He was happy to see me also.

When we went to the pizza place for lunch, another surprise happened. There was an elderly woman sitting there and, after a few moments of wondering why I knew her, she told Marina that I was a close friend of her late sister. I then recognized Alva, and we embraced and cried together just the way we did when her sister Letty passed away. Now that I had lost someone close, she felt my pain. What a wonderful reconnection with some old friends!

The waiter spoke fluent English, and he shared with me that he had been in the rehab center where both you and I had volunteered several years ago. So some more memories were kindled from our time in Baja.

Today I had my favorite breakfast at Marina's restaurant. Marina took the time to sit with me and we had a nice conversation.

The Bougainvillea we transplanted there from our house was in full bloom. I saw again, as I saw some time ago in the rose garden, that the flowers come and go, but the plant itself is not sad about it. We as spiritual Beings bring forth bodies that come and go, but our higher Self, our true Being, is ever present Life. So why are we so sad when someone lets go of the body? Possibly a false concept of Life? But how do we know if the flowers don't get sad when the neighboring one is through blooming?

What a surprise the other day when I talked to my sister and she also mentioned a concept of flowers coming and going and us being likewise! For her to express thoughts like that was a big step for her. I guess as we get older, perhaps we all start thinking more about parting with our bodies.

When returning home from breakfast, friends came to visit, and I shared with them some of my stories from the last year. Interestingly, one had some experience working with Alzheimer's patients. She understood quite well what I had been through. They both realized how difficult my visit here in Baja was but encouraged me not to make any final decisions right now.

Alberto finished the south deck and the garage roof; it all looks beautiful and the wood is protected. Josefina came for a visit in the afternoon. We had a nice time talking about future plans of renting out this beautiful house.

"Petra, focus on all the good that is happening rather than the times when I feel alone here," I tell myself. It helps during the day, and I get a few things accomplished. Today I even cooked a large pot of the squash soup that Josefina likes so much. Later on I fixed and cleaned a garage window, something I thought I couldn't do myself. By consciously encouraging myself to do these things, I find myself feeling so much better afterward. After all, we choose what we want to focus on, and today I made some good choices.

I still see so many things here that need to be done before I can rent this place, and it seems like a great mountain in front of me. But I hope that all will be accomplished during our next visit.

I'm being asked by several of my friends if I want to live here again. That is a big question. I do and I don't because right now I feel so alone here, and without you it is not a home anymore. Nature here is still as beautiful as it always was. The full moon gloriously came out of the Sea of Cortez the other day, and now the night sky before the **moonrise** is absolutely breathtaking.

One of our neighbors got sick yesterday, and today I got it also. I think I needed to experience being so sick and alone here, for it became clear to me that at this time of my life it is not wise to live so isolated. If something should happen to me here and no help is available, my children would never forgive me. I think it isn't fair to them. So right now I see my place is in the States; and this lovely house, hopefully, will be a rental income or be successfully sold someday. Someone in this world should experience the joy we have had here, and the Universe of Love knows who that is.

My special Mexican friends came by this afternoon and brought me electrolytes. They take good care of me, and I love them dearly.

Dearest Beto,

I'm back in California.

Today I would like to tell you about a very interesting development. Several weeks ago, Susanna told me about the website afterlifetv.com, and on it we watched an interview with a woman, Natalie Sudman, who had been in Iraq, hit by a roadside bomb, and had a very interesting near-death experience. Wow! We both were very impressed and taken by it, for it was quite different from any other near-death accounts we had read about. Susanna also gave me a copy of her book, *Application of Impossible Things*, which I devoured and was fascinated with, for it resonated with some of my experiences in this lifetime.

One Sunday after coming home from the Center for Spiritual Living, I was eager to dive back into the book, but a little voice said, "Why don't you give her a call since you desire to talk to her." "Sure," I replied, remembering a business number on her website and thinking, "Nobody will answer the phone because it is Sunday." So I felt confident and dialed. After a couple of rings she answered, "This is Natalie".

I was so stunned and said, "You mean you are

there?" Well, a long, wonderful conversation followed, and at the end she mentioned that she was glad to have answered the phone on a Sunday, which she normally does not do, but hearing that her writings were helping me with the grief was a wonderful gift to her.

Through her we, Susanna and I, also found out about the Monroe Institute in Virginia, where a very interesting way of balancing the right and left brain is being practiced. Also, one can have extraordinary happenings, including out-of-body experiences. Well as you know, that kind of stuff is very intriguing to me, and I dared to enroll in one of their workshops, which was held in Santa Barbara, California. Oh my! Am I glad I did that, for just as Natalie Sudman's book helped me with my grieving about your departure from this life, so did the journey with the Monroe Institute. And yes, as you know, you and I connected in two of the exercises. What a blessed gift!

This experience and other exploring journeys into spirituality are bringing me back into harmony with my life, and harmony is heaven. They are bringing me back, closer to you, to the Beingness, the **Consciousness** we are and always have been.

Dearest Beto,

It is May already, and I have not written to you; sorry, but I was in Baja, preparing our house for vacation renters or a possible sale. Originally I had planned three weeks for it; however, it turned into almost three months. Even though it was challenging at times, the greater part was healing--which you, my beloved, helped me to experience. Thank you so very much for your gentle presence!

The most important comfort I received happened when I finally, after one month being there, dared to take a walk on the beach. The tide was low, and when I got halfway to the water, I was overcome with a wave of grief, for *we* used to walk there together, and I missed you so much. But before I could let the tears roll, I felt a presence to my right, like an energy field, and then I actually heard you, my dear: "Please, don't cry, I am right here with you on your side!" Oh my, what a powerful experience that was.

So I answered, "All right, I trust you, I can feel you, and I will hold back the tears." So we walked together again, only in a different way.

When some tears did emerge later, you gave me

the message, "I know it is harder for you, for you cannot see me, but I can see you."

A little further down the shore I saw a small hermit crab that rolled with every little wave, then rolled back on its feet to hurry back towards the water. It reminded me of the advice my counselor gave me, to go with the wave of grief and not to resist it. Well, after several rolls, that little creature showed me another way to choose, for she dug into the sand firmly, and the next wave did not move her. So I reasoned that I also could choose something different, namely, to dig deeper into spirituality, into understanding the life that is beyond the physical body, and the waves of grief can roll over me but not affect me. I thought you would like my big lesson from that little crab.

After that walk on the beach with you, I felt a change in myself, and the next six weeks were much easier for me. I felt your presence often, and I talked a lot with you, even though I could not see you. I hope I was not too hard on you with my not so happy remarks when sorting things out in the garage, which used to be your territory. Well, it's all cleaned up and sorted out, and now . . . you have to send guests that will enjoy the place on their vacations or another happy couple that wants to buy it and experience their heaven on earth.

At the end of my visit, I was tempted to stay, for I felt happy being there again, especially after one morning when the dolphins came by. The sea was calm like glass. As they were gliding smoothly through the water, the early morning sun's reflection in the little ruffles around them, made them look like they were covered in sparkling diamonds. Our Mexican friends would like me to stay, but I still think it's not wise to be there permanently by myself.

One reason I wanted to be back by May was a gathering of a grief support group that had invited Hollister Rand, a medium, to work with us. It was an interesting event, for Hollister is an excellent spiritual reader. You and Pablo came through, and I think our Nico cat showed up also.

You see, I am digging deeper and trust myself to make progress in that direction, to find again the heaven on earth, the harmony and joy within my consciousness, and feel our oneness more vividly again.

Recently I found the affirmations you, my dear Beto, used to work with. Here is the copy of them:

Two little words - with great Power!

I AM.

I AM-One with Divine Consciousness, one with God.

I AM-Goodness, mercy, compassion and understanding.

I AM-Peace, joy and light.

I AM-Forgiveness, patience, strength and courage.

I AM-A helper in time of need, a comfort in time of sorrow.

I AM-A healer in time of injury, a teacher in times of confusion.

I AM-The deepest wisdom and the highest truth, the greatest peace and the grandest love.

My every thought, word, and deed emanates from divine Love.

My Immortal Beloved, yes, you are indeed all that and more! To have been in your presence for seventeen years in this human experience and, being blessed with those divine qualities, you have been and still are the greatest gift which God, Divine Love, has bestowed upon me. Thank you for all You Are!

In deepest love and gratitude,
Your wife,
Petra

P.S. This morning the thought presented itself that perhaps our former home could serve as a center of respite for tired caregivers. Wouldn't that be a blessing?! Well, "A right idea brings its own supply." I was told this once, and I have experienced it to be true. So I release that idea to the Universe of Love, and know I will be guided in the **creation of this idea to be manifested.**

Important Information

Relationships and Alzheimer's disease **caregiving** are not easy tasks. My journey through both of them have inspired me to look higher into spiritual viewpoints that sustained me in this life.

My hope is that some of my experiences and insights may be of help to some dear citizens on this planet who are faced with such a challenging opportunity for growth in grace.

The statistics report that a high number of dementia caregivers pass on before the patient, which shows how difficult this job is. Thanks to the many angels I met who supported me and also the spiritual lessons I learned during this time, I was not included in that percentage. So may others be spared from the Alzheimer Monster, that's the name I gave it, by zooming out into higher, clearer views, instead of being consumed by it.

Caregivers

Asking for help is very important! I wish I would have done that earlier than I did.

Have relatives and friends not only come and visit, or take the two of you out for a meal or ice cream but, also, let them do your job for a few days or weeks, so you get some rest away from it all. That way they might get a more accurate perspective of the situation. According to some of the experts I've met, when Alzheimer patients are outside the home, in a restaurant or family event, they behave quite normally. A different part of the brain is used for social behavior, they said.

Resources

The Alzheimer's Association.

Local caregiver support groups.

The Council on Aging.

The DVD "Communication" Series, *Caring for Someone with Alzheimer's Disease* is available through **www.medifecta.com**. Written and directed by Marion Karpinsky, RN. Get especially Volume 3 and Volume 5.

If the patient is a Veteran, please ask at the VA for all the help you can get. They have social workers to assist. Ask if the patient qualifies for "Aid in Attendance." Also find out about their Respite program.

In the Bay Area check out the OATS, Older Adults Transitional Services, a program at the El Camino Hospitals in Mountain View and Los Gatos.

Look for Alzheimer Day Activity Centers.

Family Caregiver Alliance, National Center on Caregiving, 785 Market Street, Suite 750, San

Francisco, CA 94103, 800-445-8106 or 415-343-3388, info@caregaiver.org.

Acknowledgements

My expression of deep gratitude goes to all the "Angels" who came to my side during the most difficult years of my life. Special thanks to my son Daniel who was present at the most crucial moments. I witnessed your love for my Beto in the emergency room. Before you left that night I heard you thanking him for being so dear to your mother.

The VA hospital in Palo Alto, California, is filled with Angels. Dr. Peter Lee, Dr. Lisa Tenover, all the social workers, the ER staff, and the Hospice staff; I cannot thank you enough for your compassion, kindness, and expertise.

When I had to make 911 calls, the Campbell Fire Department Angels appeared. Captain Matt Yost, you took the time and helped me to understand that I could not do the job myself anymore.

The Alzheimer's Activity Center in San Jose has Angels as Staff. Grace Tumah, how can I ever thank you enough for the help you provided for me. Beto loved you, because you are Love in action. Amy Hurst, gracias for trusting me with the DVD that helped so very much in caring for my husband, and thanks also for your patience with my frustrations.

For the generosity of Marion Karpinski, R.N., the writer and director of the DVD, I express my deepest gratitude.

Thanks be to the caregiver support group led by Tiffany Mikles. Oh, what a blessing you are to us caregivers, dear Tiffany. You also helped save my life by referring me to the OATS program at El Camino Hospital Los Gatos.

The Angel Staff at the OATS program brought me back into life through their counseling and teaching. Special thanks to my counselor Beverly, who succeeded to lift me out of the deep depression I didn't even know I had slipped into.

San Carlos Elms, the second care facility for my husband, is packed with angelic workers. What a blessing to know that it is possible for a human organization to spill over with love. Thank you, administrator Scott Evans, assistant June Wider, supervisor Ana Angulo, and all you dear, dear nurses on the Grove (the Alzheimer's unit), to let us experience true caring.

Then of course the Alzheimer's Association with the Angels of His Presence, is beyond words. You are a rock in the caregiver's community!

Last, but not least, I would like to thank my dearest friend Susanna. Oh what a blessing we are to each other in this lifetime.

In regard to the book, my gratitude goes to Ann Thompson, who cracked open my limiting shell of fear about writing, while attending her Memoir Writing Class.

More thanks to Neale Donald Walsch with his wisdom and love for humanity, who thinks everybody can and should write. Being encouraged by you helped me over the remaining blocks of limitations.

My gratitude to Mary Myers, my editor, who diligently assisted me and supported me in publishing this book.

My deep appreciation to Miko Radcliffe, graphic design artist, who took my vision of the book cover and created the expression of my heart.

Rev. Dr. Sharon Lund gave a presentation at the Center for Spiritual Living, and I consider meeting her as one of my greatest privileges. Her most interesting experience in this life after dying and what she has accomplished since, which includes Sacred Life Publishers™, makes her a Super Angel. Working with you to publish my little book proves to me that this is a Divine Adventure. Thank you so very much for your Being! You indeed are helping me to bring something "From my Heart--to Print--to Humanity."

About the Author

Petra Gerda Paul

Petra Gerda Paul came into this lifetime two months after her father was killed in WWll. Even as a child she contemplated often about life and death. As a teenager her chosen verse from the German translation of the Bible was, Psalm 90:12: "Lord, teach us to make each day count, to reflect on the fact that we must die, and so become wise."

Her life was dedicated to service. As a youngster she worked in an orphanage and hospitals. After graduating as a medical nurse in Germany she worked as head nurse of Obstetrics in Aachen, then at the Surgical University Clinic Tuebingen, as staff nurse on the Neurosurgical Unit.

In 1965 she went on the great adventure of immigrating to the United States. After two years on the East Coast she crossed the country to San Francisco, where she encountered her first metaphysical experiences by studying Christian Science.

Petra met her first husband, the father of her son, Daniel, in San Francisco. She opened her home to Foster Children for several years. One of her foster daughters Elizabeth is still very close to her. They have been a great support to each other over the years.

When the children got involved with swim teams, she also joined an adult team, to overcome the limited belief of being a total flop in sports. She developed as a long-distance swimmer and swam the length of the Golden Gate Bridge. When she participated in a Lake Tahoe crossing, she found great comfort that the Indians called the beautiful lake The Smile of the Great Spirit. After swimming in the lake for seven hours, the physician marveled that Petra's hands and body didn't suffer from the cold water.

Her interest in books about near death experiences as well as writings of inspirational writers, opened her thought to higher consciousness and brought her into universal explorations of spirituality. Whenever wisdom inspires us, it blesses and lifts the human family into the consciousness of Love.

CPSIA information can be obtained at www.ICGtesting.com
Printed in the USA
LVOW05s1249260913

354267LV00004B/236/P